MW00618573

I'm a
MESS

ASK ANYONE

Alice,
Life gets
messy,
stay close to Jesus.
♡ Pam

Life Lessons Learned From a Loving God

PAM DAVIDSON

TWO PENNY
PUBLISHING

Scriptures are taken from the Holy Bible, New International Version,® NIV.®
Copyright © 1973, 1978, 1984, 2011 by Biblica, Inc.™ Used by permission of
Zondervan. All rights reserved worldwide. www.zondervan.com. The "NIV" and
"New International Version" are trademarks registered in the United States Patent and
Trademark Office by Biblica, Inc.™

For permission requests and ordering information, email the publisher at:
info@twopennypublishing.com

FIRST EDITION

Paperback: 978-1-950995-65-3
Ebook available

Library of Congress Control Number: 2022905448

For my husband, Michael,

I am so thankful God brought us together.
Through the years, you have always helped
me with whatever "mess" I'm in.
Love you forever!

Table of Contents

Preface

Recently, our women's Bible study group focused on the book of James. Although we had studied the practical advice from James several times before, once again, the Holy Spirit revealed new insight. How? Because God's Word is living. The Holy Spirit uses the Word to convict us. 2 Timothy 3:16. "All scripture is God breathed and is useful for teaching, rebuking, correcting and training in righteousness." I was convicted to do more to put my faith into action.

A few months earlier, we studied the book of Esther. Of course, the verse that comes to mind is, "for such a time as this." Mordecai pleads with Esther to approach the king to save the Jewish people. He points out that God's plan had brought her to be the queen, and perhaps she was in that position for such a time as this.

At this point in my life, I felt compelled to take action. I asked God how else I could bring praise and glory to His name. What other avenues should I pursue to build His kingdom? In my mind, I knew God had allowed me to continue to be on earth for a reason. Without a doubt, I know our purpose revolves around ways to bring others to Christ.

The Holy Spirit continued to nudge me and after much prayer, I came to the conclusion that I should write this book. My main goal is to encourage others to have a closer relationship with Jesus.

Introduction

Imagine this story: once there was a young couple with two beautiful elementary age girls. They lived on a lovely, wooded street, and the husband had a secure job with eight years experience. Their girls attended a school within walking distance from their home, and the mom also had a well-paying job. The icing on the cake was they attended a church with a loving family of fellow Christians.

Then one day, they chose to turn their world upside down. They loaded a U-Haul truck with all their earthly possessions and moved to a new city. Perfectly ordinary, right? The extraordinary part of this life-changing event is one simple fact, neither the husband nor the wife had a job waiting for them. Let me add one caveat; the husband hadn't been fired from his job. He chose to leave. Plus, the temporary housing they expected was no longer available when they arrived. Ridiculous, right?!?! What would cause this couple, who otherwise would be considered intelligent, to make such an irrational decision?

Isaiah 6:8
"Then I heard the voice of the Lord saying,
'Whom shall I send? And who will go for us?'
And I said, 'Here am I. Send me!'"

My husband heard God's call to go into the preaching ministry. Now you might be thinking, a young couple who probably grew up in Christian homes and attended church all their lives now had the desire to go into full-time ministry. Wonderful, and may God bless them. However, that is not the real story. My husband was a new Christian, as in a two-year-old Christian.

Perhaps, I should start earlier, much earlier.

chapter one

In the Beginning:
The Faith of a Child

The world I grew up in was certainly a different place: no Facebook, no internet, no handheld phones, and no personal laptop computers. Although it was only in black and white, we did have a TV, but it just had just three channels. Perhaps that was a simpler, safer time. Certainly, kids played outdoors more, and we shared mealtimes at the family dinner table consistently.

I am in the minority of people from this era in America because I'm what some call a "military brat." Dad was in the Air Force. He retired as a Master-Sergeant. That meant he was an NCO, a non-commissioned officer. Why is that important? Being raised on an Air Force base means the main prejudice you experience is not skin color; it's based on rank. As a child attending elementary school on base, my closest friends were other kids whose parents were also NCOs. Skin color never was a factor.

I remember in one of my classes, the first thing a new girl asked me was, "What's your dad's rank? My dad is a Major." After that, we did not become friends. My closest friend's dad was a Master-Sergeant just like my dad. The fact that her skin was black and mine white never entered our minds.

All things considered, I had a blessed childhood. Both my parents loved me, and I knew that throughout my life. My mother convinced me from an early age that I was smart, and she always believed in me. I grew up in a Christian home, and my mother taught me the basic tenets of our faith. My mother professed Jesus as her Lord and Savior. My dad also had been baptized and went to church as a child. Plus, my parents were married for 57 years. Subsequently, I grew up in a stable home. Yes, I definitely had a blessed childhood.

The other major factor with having a dad in military service is moving around the country. Although I must say, we didn't move as many times as some families. I was born in Tampa, FL. When I was six, Uncle Sam sent us to Alaska! (By the way, as a child, I believed I had an Uncle Sam. Please control your laughter.) This is quite reasonable when you hear my explanation. Whenever my dad brought home some pencils or notepads from work, he would tell me, "That's from your Uncle Sam." And, of course, I believed everything my dad told me.

With orders to move from Florida to Alaska, my poor mother was sure we would freeze to death. But, as a seven-year-old, I thought being sent to Alaska was an adventure. In the summer, kids could play outside until midnight. The sun was still shining. My mother was pregnant at the time of our move. My sister, Pat, was born at the Fairbanks hospital during the first year we were there.

At first, I thought all the neighborhood kids were extra friendly until I discovered that they mostly liked to hear my southern accent. With my mother being raised in Georgia, I had picked up her southern twang. Much of my language continues to be influenced by my heritage.

All the kids walked to school, even in 40 degrees below, dressed in red or blue parkas, hoods up, scarfs covering our faces to protect our lungs, and with about five layers of clothing. Walking home, we looked a lot like wobbling penguins. Mother said that as she watched out the kitchen window, she couldn't tell which kid was hers until I walked up to the door.

After a couple of years in the far north, we moved to Idaho. The Air Force base was located on a desert plateau. We spent seven years surrounded by gray sagebrush and gray painted housing. Now, don't get me wrong, Idaho has many beautiful places. Uncle Sam chose this area because of the weather and large flat surfaces to land airplanes, I suppose. Oh, how I missed green trees! On the weekends, my dad would take us up into the mountains, a two-hour drive, and we would spend the whole day having a beautiful picnic. In the winter, we went up to the mountains to go sledding.

We were not a family that regularly went to church. Under those circumstances, you might ask, "How did I learn about Jesus?" Here again, I think my story might be unique. Because living on an Air Force base is a safe environment, kids could run and play all over the neighborhood. (Note: NCO housing.)

While attending the elementary school on base, the school bus would drop us off at a neighbor's apartment, each Wednesday afternoon. A very special lady would teach us Bible stories using flannelgraph figures. I don't remember the exact number of kids, but her living room was packed. Kids squeezed onto the couch. Some sat on the floor, side to side, knee to knee while some of us stood behind the couch. We would sing songs and choruses. I remember, specifically, she would tell part of Paul's story as told in the book of Acts. Each week she stopped the story at a cliffhanger event: Paul in jail or when he had just been beaten. Then after a little snack, she would tell a story of a missionary working somewhere around the world. She described the dangers and hardships they faced. I was in awe of these dedicated people who traveled to primitive areas, telling people about Jesus. I could hardly wait until next Wednesday.

Through her narrative of the gospel, I set my heart on how I could belong to Jesus. I developed a passion to want Him to know how much I loved Him. But how? Attending a chapel on a military base is quite different from attending most churches in the city. On base, the chapel was a building where several religions could meet and worship: Catholic, Jewish, and Protestant. People didn't join the chapel; you simply attended whichever service you wanted.

Accordingly, I couldn't join the Protestant part of the chapel. On a military base, the chapel did not operate as a civilian church. In a typical Protestant church, when you wanted to officially join the congregation, you would go forward at the end of the worship service. Then repeat your confession of faith in Jesus Christ and be baptized.

I would need to decide which Protestant church I would like to join, meaning a civilian church. Several of my friends belonged to the Baptist church, and some belonged to a Methodist church. My Dad was raised in the Christian Church in Wenatchee, Washington. My grandmother still lived there. This seemed to be a good choice for me. For this reason, we planned to travel eight or nine hours to visit my grandmother. At the same time, I could be baptized. My grandmother talked to the minister at the church and set the date.

It was a massive church with a large congregation. I don't remember much about the Sunday morning service. All I remember is standing in the baptistry, taking a glance at the audience; I saw a massive sea of faces. Subsequently, at age ten, I started my walk with Jesus which has evolved into a lifetime relationship.

Upon returning to base, I ran to tell all my friends and especially my neighbor who taught the Wednesday afternoon Bible stories, "Now I belong to Jesus!" I quickly started my own Bible story group, making my own flannelgraph figures. I cut my drawings out of paper and glued them on a small piece of flannel. Then, with a larger piece of flannel draped across the front of our TV, I would place a cutout figure on the cloth as I told a Bible story to my neighborhood friends. Now, I was the teacher, telling my friends about Jesus. I was showing Jesus how much I loved Him.

My family found a small Christian Church in a nearby town, and we started attending weekly services. What a special experience it was. We had our own church family. When I turned thirteen, I joined their youth group. For the next two years, I experienced what it was like to live close to a small town and attend a civilian church.

However, this special time came to an end all too soon. As rosy as this memory was, a dark cloud developed. You probably picked up on how I pretty much idolized my dad. But, of course, many girls do. One Sunday night at a youth group, my dad acted a little strange. Then in the middle of the lesson, he got up and rushed out of the room. He was sick. He barely got to the bathroom before he threw up. I didn't realize what was going on, and I remember being confused. My mom had to explain that dad was drunk. His sickness was alcohol.

In truth, he was an alcoholic. This fact was hidden from me because he had been sober for about five years. What changed? What caused him to "fall off the wagon?" I still don't know. I just knew that my world caved in. With my adolescent mind, I thought I must be the only teenager with an alcoholic father. Naively, I asked him to please stop drinking. Of course, he said he would, but he couldn't.

At that critical point, Uncle Sam decided that my dad should be transferred to Georgia. I had just finished my freshman year in high school. Once again, we lived on base. I rode the school bus into town for high school. It was a much larger city, and the demographics in middle

Georgia were quite different from Idaho. Until that time, I had not experienced racial prejudice. I started high school in 1963, which was the first year of full integration in schools. I hated this high school, the lack of discipline, the crowds, the smoking in the back halls, plus who knows what else. In addition to all this, the school mascot was: "The Demons!" I'm not making this up! They had a 10 ft red statue of the Demon in the main hall!

When I got home from school, I told my mother that the atmosphere seemed as if the "Demon" permeated the halls. So many black students hated the white students and vice versa. Looking back, I can now understand, with that initial transition of integration, the teachers' dilemma. How could they control the situation without causing a riot?

Each afternoon, my mom would patiently listen to my complaining. I didn't have any close friends, and I didn't like the lack of discipline, I didn't like the atmosphere. One time in my biology class, I remember a kid grabbed my test paper to copy it. The teacher did nothing as the kids laughed. Unfortunately, my family couldn't do much about the school situation. They didn't have Charter Schools or School Choice at that time. I was stuck.

We didn't attend the base chapel, and for some reason, we didn't look for a civilian church. We just didn't attend. My dad continued to drink too much. In truth, he ended up in the base hospital because of his excessive drinking. The doctor told him he was killing himself. One time I asked my mom, "Why do you put up with his drinking?" She said, "Because I love him, maybe someday you will understand."

My faith was certainly challenged. I remember thinking, "I want out of this school away from being hurt by my dad."

You need to know, my dad was not a mean drunk; his alcohol addiction was breaking my heart.

> At the end of every chapter, I want to share the lesson from God I learned through this season of my life. I hope you can see the lesson woven through my story. Let it encourage you in your story! God is always working in big and small ways in our life. Everything that we go through is meant to teach us.

KEY BIBLE VERSE

Matthew 13:31-32
"He told them another parable: 'The kingdom of heaven is like a mustard seed, which a man took and planted in his field. Though it is the smallest of all seeds, yet when it grows, it is the largest of garden plants and becomes a tree, so that the birds come and perch in its branches.'"

My neighbor, who taught me Bible stories using flannelgraph figures, planted the seed of the gospel in my heart. It took a long time for my faith to grow, but it was growing slowly. My mother wore a necklace with a mustard seed encased in a small clear orb. I remember looking at her necklace and being reminded of Jesus' parable.

When we moved to Georgia, my faith became stagnant. During those years, I didn't have a steady source of Bible teaching to help grow my faith. There were a few exceptions. One summer, my mother volunteered to help with the Vacation Bible School on the Air Force base. This was offered through the Protestant part of the base Chapel. She allowed me to be the "teacher." I read the teacher's guide and presented the lessons. Mother would help with managing the children. I loved it! My mother always said God gave me the talent and passion for teaching.

The lesson I hope you take away from my story is that in all seasons of our life, it is wise to feed on God's word continually. Seek out church families that will encourage you and help build your faith. God created His church as a family for a good reason.

Another comparison of the mustard seed and faith is found in Matthew 17:20, "Jesus said, 'Truly I tell you, if you have faith as small as a mustard seed you can say to this mountain, 'Move from here to there,' and it will move. Nothing will be impossible for you.'" Even though my faith was the size of a mustard seed, I continued to pray for my dad. I prayed that he would someday be able to overcome his addiction. Fast forward thirty years, and praise God my dad did overcome!

I plead with you my dear friends, plant mustard seeds. Never doubt for a moment that your encouraging words to a child, your loving service in the nursery, the coloring page you give to a preschooler, the time you spend preparing a Bible lesson for elementary kids, none of this is in vain. You are planting gospel seeds in these precious little minds. Yes, it may seem as if they are not listening. Yes, they run around, giggle, push and squirm. All the time, the seed may seem dormant. Yet, as my life shows, it is growing. I praise God for the beautiful woman who first shared the gospel with me.

Dobson's article, June 2021,
Life offers us only a few brief years to introduce our kids to Jesus Christ, and to teach them the biblical

I'M A MESS

principles on which tomorrow's civilization will depend. Their eternal destinies will rely on our fulfillment of this charge. Arrayed against us are formidable foes who hate what we hold dear. They are armed with powerful weapons that include the leftist educational establishment, the entertainment industry, the liberal courts, the pornography business, the nation's universities, the internet, and almost every center of power. Each of these entities and many more are increasingly hostile to the traditional family and to the values that once provided the foundation for Western Civilization. You—moms, dads and grandparents—are rapidly losing your progeny.

Where do we turn to find support and hope? Our best resource is with the committed, informed, dedicated, Bible-believing Church of Jesus Christ. There are tens of thousands of God-fearing pastors, churches and laymen who will come alongside you as you raise your kids.

chapter two

War Years:
Meeting Mike

God does work in mysterious ways or ways we could never imagine. So how was it with the Vietnam war raging in the 60s and 70s my dad and the man I thought I was in love with, were both serving in the Air Force in Vietnam. Although, they were not on the front lines; it was a war zone on the other side of the world.

At this point in my life God led this naïve 18-year-old to Mike. Like *so many teenagers*, my emotions were a hodgepodge of highs and lows controlled by hormones. My dad was in a war zone, my mom was under extreme stress from her husband off in a war, plus my younger sister and I drove her crazy. Not to mention that I thought I was in love with another man, or at least that's what my friends told me. "You make such a cute couple," they said.

Perhaps I should explain. As I mentioned in the previous chapter, the high school I attended didn't provide a comfortable or safe place for social events. When I did attend football games or dances, the chaperones were hardly seen. More importantly, kids were drinking and smoking. It was then that a friend told me about attending the USO (United Service Organization). The USO provides places for the military to have free entertainment and attend social activities.

At the local USO, my girlfriend and I enjoyed meeting guys in a safe environment. We were considered Junior Hostesses. Our responsibilities were to talk to the young Airmen and listen to their stories. For the most part, it was the first time these guys were away from home. They could be sent overseas at any time. In addition, adult chaperones were always present. At the USO, there was no drinking, no cursing, no touching the girls...safe.

I should confess, God gifted me with the inclination to talk to anyone. Or should I say, I think it is a gift, but others might not agree. Consequently, introducing myself to young men who were lonely was easy for me. We played board games, card games and danced to recorded music. I loved to dance! The guys knew that they were not allowed to ask our last names. We could tell them, but they couldn't ask.

As you can imagine, many girls and guys did decide to date. But you were not allowed to have a date at the USO. Instead, the couple would have to plan to go to a movie or out for pizza. Over time, I did meet a guy that had an interest in getting to know me better. He took me to the movies, and out to pizza. Great for me, free food and movies! Sometimes, he even came over to our house.

This all happened during the fall of my Senior year in high school. In late February of 1966, my dad got orders to go to Vietnam. The Airman I was dating didn't want my dad to leave without talking to him about marriage. Marriage?! What?! I wasn't sure, but he was. Then within two months, he also received orders to ship out to Vietnam. At that point, he said he didn't want to leave until he gave me an engagement ring. Everything happened so fast. Many young people I knew were going through the same thing. Date, get engaged, the guy gets shipped overseas.

In May of 1966, I graduated from high school. Not a happy time with my dad and fiancée in a war zone. Not only that, but also the high school itself had burnt down! I mean entirely to the ground in January of that year. Thank goodness the electrical fire took place during the night. No one was hurt. But my fellow students and I had to attend the rival high school across town. They went in the mornings, and we went in the afternoons. (Much later in my life, when we worked with youth groups, I had a guaranteed comeback for when the teens whined about high school. "You feel like you are having a rough time?!? During my senior year, my dad was in a war zone and our high school burnt down to the ground!" Their response, "Wow!")

During this era, it was expected that graduates either got a job, went to college, or enlisted in the military. My girlfriend, the same friend who introduced me to the USO, decided to attend an IBM business school in Atlanta, two hours from home. Since my parents couldn't afford to send me to college, I chose to follow my friend's example. At least I would be qualified for a good job after five months of training.

My poor mother was worried to death. The school was in downtown Atlanta. The "dorm" was a hotel dating from the post-civil war era. We walked the five blocks down Peachtree Street from the dorm to the school. Our meals were served in a small café across the street. This café happened to be right above a basement bar.

Talk about a reality shock! Imagine teenage girls mostly from small towns living in the BIG city amid race riots, sirens at night, and working girls coming upstairs to the café in the mornings. You see, this was the beginning of "topless go-go" girls. I think I walked around with my mouth ajar for the first few weeks.

During that time, God continued His protection. Although I never walked alone, several of us didn't think anything about walking blocks and blocks to get to a movie theater or big department store, even at night. We went home on the weekends. Even though I didn't attend church throughout these five months, I remember thinking how empty the people seemed. They needed Jesus and didn't know it.

When I completed my course of "key punch" operator (that is something you may need to look up on Google), I went back home and got a job on the Air Force base. All the while, my dad and the man whose engagement ring I wore, continued to be in Vietnam.

Then, along came Mike.

So that long-ago October day in 1966, when Ms. Fritz (one of the directors at the USO) asked me if I could help with the Halloween party, I said sure. What was strange was that Ms. Fritz <u>introduced</u> me to Mike. We were supposed to introduce ourselves. (Mike later told me that he had asked Ms. Fritz to introduce him to the nicest girl there. Hmm)

Mike did not know what he was in for! Mike is so easy to like, polite, non-assuming, and quiet. For the Halloween party, Mike was putting up some apparatus that would slide down a wire and light up. Interesting, I thought or a little weird. As days passed, Mike and a couple of other guys would come over to our house (a mobile home) and find ways to help out around the house and get a free meal. Keep in mind; my dad was still in Vietnam. Mother provided homemade pizza.

As October turned into November, I found my emotions in disarray. Why was I attracted to Mike? I <u>thought</u> I was "in love" with another guy. One time Mike and one of his buddies had taken a weekend trip to his friend's hometown. They shared about how much fun they had meeting girls and going out. In my heart, I felt jealous. What is that all about? I'm planning to marry someone else; their fun shouldn't bother me.

Don't forget that Mike and I did not go on "dates." We met at the USO and played cards and games with friends I had met since I had returned from Atlanta. Someone would pick me up and later drive me home. Most of the time, a couple of the guys would drive me. On a particular evening, Mike was the only one available to take me home. We didn't say a word to each other. As we drove on in silence it became more and more awkward. As the silence continued, the tension built until you could slice the air with a knife.

Mike pulled into a parking lot. We just looked at each other (no, really, that is all we did: look at each other.) Finally, one of us said, "What are we going to do?" We knew we were in love. At first, Mike didn't want to talk about marriage. He respected the fact that I was engaged to someone else.

Even as a very young Christian and immature teenager, my faith in God was strong. I had (and still have) total confidence in God. When we pray and ask for His direction in our lives, He will answer. James 1:5 says, "If any of you lacks wisdom, you should ask God, who gives generously to all without finding fault, and it will be given to you."

Believe me, I prayed for guidance as I had never prayed before. I asked God to help me sort out my emotions. I didn't understand my feelings. One night, in particular, I prayed for hours, "Who should I marry?" Although I can't explain it in exact words, God led me to Mike.

The next time I saw Mike was when he came over to help us wrap our water pipes because freezing weather was on its way. Remember, we lived in a mobile home, and the pipes were exposed under the house. After we finished wrapping the pipes, I took off my gloves and showed him I had taken off my engagement ring. After a long night in prayer, I told him that God answered, and I knew I should marry him.

My decision came a few days before the Christmas Mike spent with us. After Christmas, he went home to Fort

Myers, FL, for a few days. When he came back, he had his grandmother's engagement ring with him. That evening he placed it on my finger.

My dad got back from Vietnam in March 1967, with orders from Uncle Sam to move across the country in 30 days. Let's see; it went something like this. "Hi, Dad, glad you are home safe; meet Mike; we want to get married. You're right; he is a different guy than I thought I would marry; but no worries we just need to hurry up because I want you to walk me down the aisle." Again, crazy, right?

See my dilemma? How would I ever see Mike again if I moved with my family? He could get orders to go to Vietnam any day. In my mind, the only solution was to get married quickly.

My mother explained that she and dad didn't have any money to pay for a wedding. I certainly understood. (Mother confessed much later, she and my dad were concerned that if they tried to stop us, we would run off to get married in a different state. *In Georgia, an eighteen-year-old needed her parents' signatures to acquire a marriage license.*)The money issue didn't deter me. I had a job. I was making money, not a lot but enough. Talk about a "shoestring budget!"

My dress came from the Sears catalog. It was a two-piece, white lace, simple top and skirt. I asked my best friend to be my bride's maid; and her mom made her a simple a-lined pink dress. Flowers were ordered, two small bouquets, one white and one pink and corsages for my mom, my sister, Mike's mom, and my grandmother. Finally, I ordered a small cake. With my dad and Mike in the Air Force, we had the wedding ceremony in the base chapel with a chaplain, Captain Wallace. Our only expense was paying the organist. The reception was at the NCO club, very budget-friendly.

On April 2, 1967, Mike and I were married, and I was blessed to have my dad walk me down the aisle. Mike was still serving in the Air Force with three years left. After our wedding, my mom, dad, and sister moved across the country. Mike's parents, who, by the way, I met the day before our wedding, lived ten or so hours away. Mike and I found a small, cheap, concrete block apartment to rent. Our journey together began.

KEY BIBLE VERSE

James 1:5-6
"If any of you lacks wisdom, you should ask God, who gives generously to all without finding fault, and it will be given to you. But when you ask, you must believe and not doubt, because the one who doubts is like a wave of the sea, blown and tossed by the wind."

Wisdom, the world equates wisdom with success. For example, if you make a large salary, own a huge house, boat, and so on, you must be wise to have achieved such wealth. On the other hand, God's wisdom begins with, "The fear of the Lord is the beginning of wisdom; all who follow his precepts have good understanding. To him belongs eternal praise." Psalm 111:10.

While attending high school, I saw so many young people searching for wisdom and identity by imitating what they saw in the world around them. Experimenting with drinking, drugs, and sexual activities were their means of searching. It seemed no one directed them to God's wisdom. I certainly didn't. I just knew I didn't want to be like them.

During my time in Atlanta, my memory is seeing people with blank expressions on their faces. Searching for success or fame or racial identity. They certainly didn't look to God for wisdom. In my mind, I saw that they needed to know Jesus. But how to tell them??? My soul cried out, "The world is hurting. What can I do?!?"

My pursuit for wisdom came to a climax when as a young adult, I faced the life-changing decision of who I should marry. I was wrestling with my feelings for Mike. Praying to God to ask for His direction was the most logical choice.

My prayer at that time was very childlike. But God doesn't require us to be mature or perfect. When we call on Him, He hears our prayers. Mark 11:24, "Therefore I tell you, whatever you ask for in prayer, believe that you have received it, and it will be yours." God knows our hearts. When we approach His throne of grace, we simply need to have a childlike faith. Matthew 18:3, "And He said: 'Truly I tell you, unless you change and become like little children, you will never enter the kingdom of heaven.'"

James is teaching us in chapter one about God's wisdom, living your life dedicated to Him. When we face decisions in life and desire to make the right choice, we can simply ask God for His wisdom. As Christians, our goal is to live in God's will, doing the work He designed us to complete. Accordingly, when I was faced with deciding which man I should marry, I went to God in prayer.

Do you desire to live a fulfilled life? Have you searched for success and even achieved goals you may have set for yourself? Are you at peace with your decisions and walk in life? Or are you still seeking something more?

My dear friends, living for Jesus is the answer. He came that we may have life and experience life in its fullness. God created us and designed us for a purpose. Until you strive to live according to His plan, you will continue to feel empty. Bear in mind, as you face crossroads in your lives, God loves you and desires the best for you. Seek the Lord's wisdom, and He will direct your paths.

chapter three

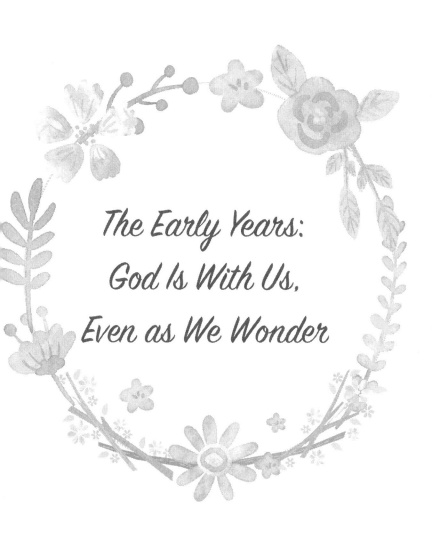

The Early Years:
God Is With Us,
Even as We Wonder

Now, what? For a few months, we attended church, meaning the chapel on base. After all, Mike told me he was a Christian, and to be fair, he thought he was. You see, Mike's grandparents took him and his brothers to a Methodist church. Mike and his brothers went through the motions and classes, and therefore, they were Christians. As soon as they were old enough to say I don't want to go, that stopped.

When one day I heard his declaration, "I don't want to go to church," it came as a shock! He went on to say, "He didn't need it." For him going to church was a "crutch," and he was fine. What?? Mike also started sharing ideas he had learned at college, a secular college that taught him, along with academics, a heavy dose of humanism. Such as, man is wise, and believing in God is pure foolishness! Anyone who needs religion is weak. One statement he made sent me reeling, "Christianity practices a kind of 'cannibalism.' Communion says you take and eat of Jesus' body and blood." WHAT? I was stunned. (I can look back now and see he said that just for shock value, and it worked. I had nothing to say.)

I couldn't believe it! What was happening? In spite of Mike's assertions, I was still convinced that God wanted me to marry Mike, but what now? Did I question my faith? You bet I did. My parents were in Oregon, and we were in middle Georgia. I didn't have anyone to talk to about Mike's ideas. As I told you, being raised on an Air Force base in the '50s and '60s equated to a very sheltered life. Mike had three years of college. He was an intelligent guy, smart, as in worldly smart.

It is amazing; I should say our God is amazing. Because as I look back on our first months of marriage, God continued to have his hand in guiding our lives. As I mentioned before, during the late '60s early '70s the Vietnam war was raging. Young airmen were being sent overseas every month from Mike's squadron. In fact, the chaplain that married us, reminded us of that very fact in one of our counseling sessions. At the department on base where Mike worked, they had a list posted of the Airmen. They were listed in the order that they arrived at the base. One by one, each of them was sent to Vietnam, pretty much in the order that they had arrived. But as each one shipped out, and names were crossed off the list, Mike's name was skipped. He didn't have to go overseas! Praise God!

Our first years together consisted of typical events of a young married couple. I got a job to help supplement our income. We were blessed with our first daughter, Melinda. Two months after her birth, I went back to work. You get the picture we were struggling financially but making it. We had the goal of Mike getting back to FSU as soon as he got out of the service to complete his senior year.

In 1970, I experienced my first taste of civilian life. My life up until this point had been living as a military dependent. Civilian life was quite the kick in the teeth! Mike attended classes at Florida State University in Tallahassee. Melinda went to daycare, and I worked every hour offered to me. Mike was in class a few hours then home the rest of the time. His goal was studying, making good grades, and earning his degree. I come home with a toddler, meals to fix, groceries to buy, laundry to do, on and on. He helped but goodness! Praise God; we made it from paycheck to paycheck.

My disposition became more and more negative. Plus, everywhere I looked, people needed Jesus. Everyone was busy either earning a paycheck or studying to make a better future for themselves. But life was empty for them and frankly fairly empty for me. People were searching but not knowing what was missing. I was muddling through. I knew

Jesus was the answer, but I didn't know how to "fit" him into this rushed life.

As I reflect on this part of our lives, I am puzzled that I didn't try to find a church to attend. I was in a downward spiral, working a job with as many overtime hours as I could get. My selfish heart was saying, "This better pay off." I had always wanted to go to college, but my parents couldn't afford it. So now I watched Mike go to classes, while I tried to figure out how many meals I could stretch one pound of hamburger into.

As for a social life, forget it. There wasn't room in the budget for fun. We simply didn't go "out." Mike's brother and sister-in-law lived in Tallahassee at the time. They were both graduates of FSU. As you can imagine, football was a big-time activity in town. My sister-in-law asked us why we didn't go to the games. The answer was simple; we couldn't afford a babysitter. Plus, I didn't attend the university; I would have to pay full price for a ticket.

As Mike graduated, the head of his department offered him an internship which, when finished, he would receive a master's degree in American Studies. But he turned it down. Our marriage couldn't take another year like this. Although I had a job with people I enjoyed working with, I was tired. My visions of married and civilian life did not equate to my reality.

I even started packing my bags one time. Not that I wanted a divorce, I just wanted to show him I had had it! See how you can make it without me! Mike reassured me that we both still loved each other, which we did. He said what was causing problems were the circumstances we were dealing with. Furthermore, he was right.

Finally, in December 1970, Mike received his bachelor's degree. Now what? Well, Mike had a hometown, Fort Myers,

FL. He got a job at a local bank, and we moved into an apartment. Being a naive 22-year-old, I thought having a college degree would mean you automatically start making the "big bucks." Guess what, I needed to go back to work. But at least we lived in a town with family close by. Having Mike's family close was a real blessing. We enjoyed many family meals together. During the next year, we were blessed with having another daughter, Christie.

Life was full. Or at least it was the picture of what our culture dictates to be successful. We were blessed with two beautiful daughters; we had just purchased our first home, and had family living nearby. Wow! I had a "hometown" for the first time in my life. It was comfortable. I remember thinking that perhaps it was time to find a church. (Remember, I hadn't experienced a close church relationship since I was 14, and that time, it only lasted two years.)

None of Mike's family attended a church, not his parents, aunt and uncle, or cousins. Nevertheless, I was determined to find a church to attend. My "requirements" were Protestant, small, and not too far to drive. Guess what? Mike even went with me.

My perception was disappointing. The preacher must have been getting ready to move to another church. His message was about what the church leaders needed to do to improve things. My heart cried out! Don't you care about the people right here in this city that need to know Christ!? Why aren't you out telling people about Jesus!? Well, Satan indeed used that experience to dampen my urge to find a church. I didn't even try for several years.

KEY BIBLE VERSE

2 Timothy 4:2
"Preach the word; be prepared in season and out of season; correct, rebuke and encourage— with great patience and careful instruction."

How can our churches stand by and ignore what is happening to our society? For too long, the church has practiced apathy. Watching evil become more and more prevalent in our world. Excuses such as: I'm only one person, what can I do; or it doesn't affect me. Perhaps some are persuaded to think, I belong to a church, we don't participate in such activities, nor do we condone them. Instead, we turn our backs and close our eyes to the growing tidal wave of immoral behavior in our culture. What's worse is we allow laws to be passed that contradict God's law.

"Apathy seems like a fairly harmless attitude, but it is much more destructive than we first think. The dictionary definition of apathy is "a lack of interest, a lack of feeling or emotion." It can come across as "I just can't be bothered," but it is a much deeper problem than that because something has switched off in our emotions caused by a hardness of heart." Quote from Scott Brennan, Coach at **Cairn Movement**, Scotland, devotion 11/2/2021

Dear friends, are you searching for opportunities to serve our Lord? Are you exploring ways to get involved in issues that the enemy is using to demoralize our culture? For example, is there a pregnancy crisis center in your area where you might be able to volunteer? Or try something as easy as looking up the website: Intercessors for America, ifapray.org.

Are you living out your faith? Do we "walk the walk" or just "talk the talk?"

"I charge you in the presence of God and of Christ Jesus, who is to judge the living and the dead, and by His appearing and His kingdom: preach the word; be ready in season and out of season; reprove, rebuke, and exhort, with complete patience and teaching. For the time is coming when people will not endure sound teaching, but having itching ears, they will accumulate for themselves teachers to suit their own passions, and will turn away from listening to the truth and wander off into myths. As for you, always be sober-minded, endure suffering, do the work of an evangelist, fulfill your ministry." 2 Timothy 4:1-5

What about you? Could you start a prayer group where you work? Perhaps, before work hours or during lunch. Perhaps, try using a prayer journal and write the names of people you know that need Jesus. Then, pray for opportunities to meet and share your love of Jesus with others. The Holy Spirit will guide you.

I remember the first time I prayed that God would lead me to someone who needed to know Jesus and to provide an opportunity, an open door. The next day at work, one of the women I shared an office with, asked me if I had read the article in the newspaper about a man who "died" in his hospital bed and was brought back with the defibrillator. The man said he saw "a bright light." My co-worker wanted to know what I thought. Well, let me tell you, my heart started pounding as I felt the Holy Spirit nudge me. Yes, I did tell her why I believe in heaven and that Jesus is the way. But, don't get too excited; she didn't jump up and exclaim, "I want to go to church." In fact, I don't know if she ever went to church or came to know Jesus. <u>But I planted a seed</u>.

chapter four

Turning Point:
Through a Child

When Melinda was four years old, a neighbor, who also had a four-year-old daughter, asked to take Melinda to church with them. (Okay, sidebar: I had not been to church for several years. I was struggling; where was God in this mixed-up world??? I continued my great love of Jesus, but going to church???) Melinda loved going with her friend, and I started to feel embarrassed that I wasn't taking her.

"Mother guilt," you know what that's like, right? "Mother guilt" has a switch that is turned on when you give birth. I don't think there is an "off" switch. Mothers feel guilt if their child gets sick, or hurt, doesn't behave well, says bad words, on and on. Even when their son/daughter goes to school, if they don't find a new friend, it must be the mom's fault. It's ridiculous, right, but there it is.

Motivated by my "mother guilt," we started attending church, just Melinda and me. Christie was a very busy toddler (4 broken bones by the time she was 5!!! But that's another story.) Melinda loved her Sunday School class, and I certainly felt loved also. As time went on, and I made close friends with my sisters in Christ, I started attending the women's ministry meetings. Now I felt comfortable. Only women were welcome, no worries if your husband didn't come to church. I didn't stand out.

Let me tell you, I grew so much through the Bible studies, service projects, fellowship, and retreats. One study, in particular, made me sit up straight:

1 Peter 3:1-2, "Wives, in the same way submit yourselves to your own husbands so that, if any of them do not believe the word, they may be won over without words by the behavior of their wives, when they see the purity and reverence of your lives."

Oh, yeah, right, "submit yourselves to your own husbands!" Really? And what about the next part of that verse? "... That they may be won over without words by the behavior of their wives." Without words! Seriously, Lord, you know me. I don't know how to do anything without words! Even when I use my words, Mike will question, "What are you trying to say?"

Hmm, I'm thinking, while Peter was writing God's message for the early Christians, he didn't realize how outrageous his words would sound two thousand years later. "Submit" is not a word our American culture uses. Instead, we have the rights that our forefathers fought for, and soldiers continue to fight wars to preserve our individual freedoms.

Now let's get things straight; I'm not a "women's libber." Let me explain. "The women's liberation movement (WLM) was a political alignment of women and feminist intellectualism that emerged in the late 1960s and continued into the 1980s primarily in the industrialized nations of the Western world, which effected great change (political, intellectual, cultural) throughout the world." (Wikipedia) I've never been one who follows fads, but the shouting and cheering for women's rights were loud. Being a 23-year-old working mom of two, I was liberated enough. Right?

Our women's group decided to study a book titled: Fascinating Womanhood, by Helen Andelin, 1971. The author's basic message was to treat your husband like a king, and he will treat you like a queen. Hmm, I know what you are thinking, "Sure, right, like that is going to work!" She suggested we remember how we felt about our husband when we first met, how handsome he was, how loving and kind. The next recommendation was to leave him "love notes" where he would find them; like in his underwear drawer. LOL, stop your laughter, because I did it! If you are ready to stop holding your sides from laughing, I'll proceed.

If you think this book has improbable ideas, let me tell you about another book that became popular about the same time. It's titled: <u>Total Woman</u> by Marabel Morgan, 1973. Although we did not specifically study this book, many women shared some ideas with the group. For example, the author states: "It's when a woman surrenders her life to her husband, reveres and worships him and is willing to serve him, that she becomes beautiful to him." One of the most memorable suggestions was for the wife to greet her husband at the door wearing a sexy outfit (like a raincoat with nothing under it!) Yeah, right, I didn't try that idea!

Add these ideas to how God is directing wives in 1 Peter chapter 3, "submit yourselves to your husbands." What to do, how to do it, submit? Obviously, pray. I confess that although I made attempts to submit to Mike, I certainly wasn't very successful.

Once again, my dear sisters in Christ helped me. I asked my sisters to pray that Mike would decide to come to church. And they did. Mike came once, but it wasn't fruitful. What was productive was my spiritual growth. Attending worship services each week helped me grow stronger in my faith. The biggest change/growth came through attending the women's Bible studies. My sisters in Christ encouraged me, prayed with me and became my mentors. I was actually studying the Bible for the first time in my life.

Then another shock about civilian life!! The bank Mike worked for transferred him to their Tampa office. What? I grew up thinking civilians stayed in one place, or if they moved, it was because they wanted to. My dream of having a hometown disappeared like a puff of smoke. After living in apartments for many years, we were enjoying our new home. Plus, I loved the church the girls and I were attending. I thought I finally had a "hometown." Now what?

First, get our home ready to sell. Check. And at the same time, make a trip to Tampa to start our home search. Check. As the realtor drove around and helped me search for homes, I continued to pray about which house would be the best choice for us. I had seen one while I was driving around by myself a few days before. It seemed to be the perfect neighborhood and price. When I met up with the realtor, we went straight to that house. Guess what? It had just been sold! My realtor was concerned that I was upset, but I told her that I had been praying about this decision. Therefore, if the house was sold, God did not intend for us to buy that one.

We continued our search in the surrounding neighborhood. The builder informed us that a house that was completed and had been under contract just came back on the market. Unfortunately, a mistake had been made; the corner of the house's garage was placed closer to the property line than it should have been. Consequently, the initial buyer canceled the contract. Plus, the builder reduced the price!

As we examined the house, I fell in love with the layout. Even with the dropped price, it was still a bit above our top price point. Mike drove up to check it out, and he agreed we should sign a contract because it was a "bargain" for that big of a house.

Meanwhile, a couple decided to buy our home in Fort Myers, and it went under contract. Everything was fitting together perfectly. A couple of weeks before the closing date on our Fort Myers house, I got a call from our realtor. The contract for the house in the Tampa area fell through. The mortgage company would not give approval to finance the new home.

Wait, Lord, what is going on! I didn't want to move in the first place. I prayed about the house before we signed the contract; I thought this was your will? After having a "hissy fit"—reality hit! We had to get out of the Ft. Myers house; people were ready to move into it. I went to Tampa to find a place to rent. I needed to get everything arranged because Mike was busy with his job. I took care of packing (praise God the bank paid our moving cost). I had to find Melinda a school; she was in first grade, get the water, electricity, etc., hooked up. Whew!

We rented a duplex with two bedrooms and one bathroom. Certainly, not what I had envisioned. But God is good all the time. One blessing within all this confusion, my parents and sister lived about 30 minutes from the duplex. So, once again, God provided a support system for us as Mike started traveling more and more frequently for the bank.

 KEY BIBLE VERSE

1 Peter 3:1-2
"Wives, in the same way submit yourselves to your own husbands so that, if any of them do not believe the word, they may be won over without words by the behavior of their wives, when they see the purity and reverence of your lives."

Dear friends, we know God's word "is living and powerful, and sharper than any two-edged sword, piercing even to the division of soul and spirit, and of joints and marrow, and is a discerner of thoughts and intents of the heart." Hebrews 4:12

I confess that the first time I read this passage in 1 Peter, I was nothing less than shocked! How could a loving God expect women to submit to their husbands? Wasn't Christianity the great equalizer? Didn't Paul say, "There is neither Jew nor Greek, there is neither slave nor free, there is no male and female, for you are all one in Christ Jesus." Galatians 3:28. So how do we reconcile that verse with what Peter is telling us? It's enough to make a girl's head spin!

Once more, God's family, especially my Christian sisters, helped guide me and teach me. We are God's creation; He knows what is best for us, but in His great love, He allows us to make free choices. From the beginning, God designed man and woman to be joined together as husband and wife. He gave us an outline for how a relationship best works.

"For the husband is the head of the wife as Christ is the head of the church, his body, of which he is the savior. Now, as the church submits to Christ, so also wives should submit to their husbands in everything. Husbands, love your wives, just as Christ loved the church and gave himself up for her…" Ephesians 5:23-25. Well, that certainly adds a different perspective. Husbands should love their wives to the point that they would be ready to die for her.

As I mentioned, our women's group was studying the book, Fascinating Womanhood; my opinion was that the author's suggestions would work for women married to Christian men. How could this help my relationship with Mike? I did try a few of her ideas, like leaving love notes and of course, Mike responded well. But that didn't bring him any closer to wanting to know Jesus.

Back to God's Word. As I reread the verses in 1 Peter chapter 3, my heart was pierced. God's Spirit led me to a new view. Did I love Jesus with all my heart and soul? Yes. Did I desire to live for Jesus in all areas of my life? Yes. Did I choose to submit my life to God's will? Yes. Did I love Jesus enough to submit to Him? Yes. Well, then, that meant I must learn to submit to my husband.

Even with this conviction, my will and ego continued to fight against this submission idea. I believe it is a lifelong struggle. Confession time again, I had moments where I was able to obey God, and then I had plenty of other times where my ego/pride got in the way.

Dear friends, may I encourage you to continue to read God's word and then reread God's word. Then, when dealing with a confusing thought or an idea you don't agree with or seems confusing, seek a friend. Part of God's eternal plan for His church is that we become a family. We need each other; we help each other grow in our faith.

Finally, remember, "All scripture is God-breathed and is useful for teaching, rebuking, correcting and training in righteousness, so that the servant of God may be thoroughly equipped for every good work." 2 Timothy 3:16-17.

chapter five

Walking a Fine Line: Holding onto My Faith and Loving My Husband

Once again, we were in an apartment, well, a duplex, actually. But all things considered, it was comfortable. There was one factor that made this location <u>memorable</u>: the train. Out our back sliding glass doors within a stone's throw, the freight train heading into Tampa came about every 15 minutes.

These were the days before TVs had remote controls. Subsequently, every time the train went through, we couldn't hear the TV. By the time you could get up and turn the volume up, the train was gone. Ugh! During the night, we learned to sleep through it. One day when my grandmother was visiting, she and the girls were at the dining room table when I needed to go next door for a moment. I came back in just as a train was passing. My poor grandmother's eyes were as big as saucers!

After the dust settled, we found a routine. Melinda could ride her bike to school since it was so close. And praise God, I didn't need to go back to work right away. Christie was three years old and kept me <u>busy</u>. (Remember, she's the one who had four broken bones by the time she was five. Fearless was her middle name.) For my sanity, I found a daycare for Christie to attend, just one day a week. This arrangement was good for both of us; plus, we were close enough to my parents' home to visit often. Okay, God, we're good.

Except for Mike's duties at the bank required him to travel during the week. Finally, he spent so much time at the bank's Jacksonville office; they arranged housing for him. As a result, he was only home on the weekends. He would get home late on Friday nights and leave Sunday nights. Consequently, taking the girls to church every Sunday morning drastically cut into his visit time.

Mike continued his stance of not needing a church or religion. I was walking a fine line, spending time with my husband, and making sure our girls learned about Jesus. As well as that, I needed the Christian fellowship. One morning, I opened the mail . Mike sent me a letter from Jacksonville. The main part of it read something like, "I hope you know what you are doing to our girls. I don't think I can continue to be in a marriage where I am not important to you." Well, knock me over with a feather!

My selfish heart cried out, "Are you kidding me? I followed you to Florida State University; I was the one working to get you through your senior year! Then I followed you to Fort Myers. I went back to work to help support our family. I loved having a "hometown." Finally, I followed you to Tampa! And you say my actions don't show you how important you are?"

At this point in my life, I was still so young in my faith. What should I do? After praying, I called Mike, right then, right there, in the middle of the day, while he was working at the bank! Okay, so I'm a bit impulsive...sometimes a lot impulsive. I told him that I loved him with all my heart, but I also loved Jesus, and I am not willing to give him up or Jesus! (That showed him! Right???) Pretty much Mike didn't quite know what to say. Hmm...

My Mom was so discerning. After telling her about Mike's letter, she had a great suggestion. Wise in her years, she knew Mike was jealous of me spending time away from him by attending church on the weekends, during the only time he was home. She suggested I fly to Jacksonville and spend a long weekend with Mike. The girls would stay with my parents.

Praise God! Mike and I had a wonderful weekend (after I recovered from my nausea from a very bumpy flight. Mike even commented, "Your green skin color doesn't go well with your pink pantsuit." Ha-ha). He enjoyed showing me around the city and I enjoyed his gratified attitude. Mother was right, and yes, I did tell her.

Our marriage relationship was better, but I continued to walk that fine line. Sundays continued to be a strain. I would have loved to go to the first hour, which consisted of adult Bible study, and then the second hour that was worship, but that was pushing my time away from Mike.

By mid-summer, we had been in the apartment for about five months. At that time, we hit another bump in the road. Mike's bank decided he needed to be at the Jacksonville office full time. What?!? Move again?!?

KEY BIBLE VERSE

Ruth 1:16-17

"Entreat me not to leave you, Or to turn back from following after you; For wherever you go, I will go; And wherever you lodge, I will lodge; Your people shall be my people, And your God, my God. Where you die, I will die, And there will I be buried. The Lord do so to me, and more also, If anything but death parts you and me."

When Chaplain Wallace officiated our wedding, he read this passage from Ruth. Although in these verses, Ruth is speaking to her mother-in-law Naomi, Chaplain Wallace applied the vow to marriage.

The story of Ruth is a beautiful love story. It's a story of faith, devotion, trust, humility, and deep love. Remember, Ruth was a Moabite. Her culture worshiped idols. After she married Naomi's son, she must have learned from her mother-in-law about our true God.

Ruth was an amazing woman. After her husband died, she chose to stay with Naomi. Remember, at this time in history, women didn't have a way to support themselves. They were dependent on their husbands or sons. After Naomi's husband and other son died, she made the decision to go back to her homeland. Incredibly, Ruth decided to follow her.

Now Ruth is in a foreign country. She had to adapt to a new culture, new language, and she was from Moab. Her home country was considered enemies with Naomi's home country. I am amazed by Ruth's courage as we read how she obeyed the directives Naomi gave her.

Ruth's life story ends like a fairy tale. A handsome man falls in love with her. He saves not only Ruth, but also Naomi. Let me not fail to mention, because of Ruth's faith and obedience; she is listed in Jesus' lineage!

Although in most cases of marriage today, our culture doesn't reflect the love and dedication of Ruth. And certainly, I didn't consider myself in any sense in the league of Ruth. But my heart's desire was to remain married. I continually reflect on my prayer, asking God's guidance about who to marry. I had no doubts that God intended Mike and I to be married.

My dear friends, please remember, life's circumstances can weaken us and allow the enemy to distract and misdirect our paths. "Trust in the Lord with all your heart and lean not on your own understanding." Proverbs 3:5

Ruth could have stayed in her homeland, which would be a safe option. But she didn't let a set of circumstances intimidate her; she trusted in God. Remember, "Look to the Lord for his strength, seek His face always." Psalm 105:4

chapter six

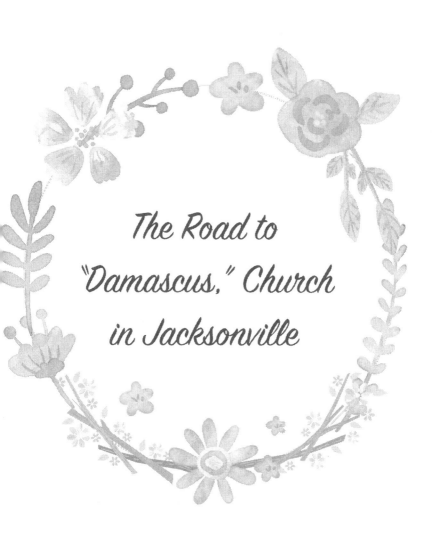

*The Road to
"Damascus," Church
in Jacksonville*

Once again, I journeyed to a new city to find a place for us to live. Seriously, I was a bit confused with God's plan for our lives. When God led me to the church in Fort Myers, where I refocused my faith, I believed I had a hometown and church. How would God work this move out for His purpose? I had no clue at the time.

As I grew in my faith, I turned my prayers towards Mike. After a while, I could see the church in Fort Myers wasn't the place for Mike to make a connection to God. Importantly, when we moved to the Tampa area, I prayed that we would find the circumstances that would lead Mike to Christ. Instead of Mike coming closer to God, we experienced a serious situation in our marriage. With Mike traveling and being gone all week and my desire to continue to attend church on Sunday, he felt unloved and ignored. Our relationship healed after my trip to Jacksonville to focus on him and our love for each other. Now facing another move, my prayer was, "Please help us find a church home where someone would be able to touch Mike's heart for Christ." My prayers also included my need to find another place to experience a close fellowship.

After learning our lesson about mortgage financing, I was more cautious with the price. With assistance from the bank, we contacted a realtor. Jacksonville is a huge city, and I needed help navigating the area. So, we narrowed the search to a location within an easy commute to Mike's work.

At this time, there wasn't a large selection of homes for sale in the area we were zoned in on. After a weekend of searching (yes, only one weekend), we narrowed our choice down to three houses. I liked a newly built little house in an older neighborhood. It was a beautiful tree-lined, quiet street. Most homes were 50 to 80 years old. A builder bought an undeveloped lot in a great location, and added two houses.

The house was close to the elementary school and the main avenue. Resale value never entered my mind. I would discover a few years later, buying a newly constructed house in an older neighborhood would/could mean a tough resale.

Our move went smoothly. So many new neighbors dropped by to welcome us, some with baked goodies! It made me wonder if it had been a long time since someone new moved into the neighborhood. There was one other young family that lived on our street, which was nice because they had two elementary-age kids. Melinda, age seven, and Christie, age three, had new friends.

In my mind, after getting Melinda registered in school, my next task was to find a church. So we visited Englewood Christian Church right away. It was the nearest Christian church to our new home.

Englewood had a larger congregation than I had experienced, but the people and atmosphere were very warm and welcoming. Melinda loved her new Bible school teacher, Mrs. Smith, the preacher's wife.

I joined the church right away. It was usual practice for the preacher to visit new members as soon as possible; therefore, I had expected him to drop by. But when Fred Smith came to visit our home one evening, the conversation took an unexpected turn.

Mike was sitting on one chair, I was on the opposite side of our small living room, and Fred was in the middle on our couch. The evening began with a bit of small talk, "Where are you from? Why did you move to Jacksonville, etc." I told Fred about how our girls and I attended a small church in Fort Myers and one just outside of Tampa. Mike explained that his job required us to move to the area.

Fred's next question nearly knocked me over! He turned to Mike and asked him what his church background was. What? Wait! I could feel and see the hair on the back of Mike's neck go up. Mike's entire body went rigid. Mike simply said he was raised in the Methodist church. Although I had prayed for someone to reach out to Mike; this was certainly unexpected timing!

Mike had not even visited the church yet. Also, I had not told Fred about Mike. In my mind, I cried out, no, wait! Consequently, I jumped into the conversation to deflect the arrows Mike's eyes directed toward Fred. "Mike considers me a bit of a fanatic about the church," I giggled.

Fred was not deterred. In the conversation that followed, Fred simply laid out the gospel. How Christ came, died for our sins, and became our righteousness. This time, I just sat quietly.

After Fred left our home, Mike turned to me and accused me of asking Fred to confront him, specifically. I told him, "No way, I wouldn't do that!" But no matter how hard I tried, Mike was convinced this visit was staged by me. (Much later, we found out that Fred rarely, if ever, presents the gospel on his first visit to a home. The Holy Spirit simply led him to do so on this occasion.)

When the next Sunday arrived, I told the girls to very quietly get ready for church. We didn't want to bother or wake daddy. A few weeks later, as the girls and I followed our quiet routine, Mike got up and dressed for church. Wow! Super!

In fact, he started coming weekly. Oh, my goodness, could this be happening? Let me add a little detail; throughout the sermon Mike would repeatedly glance at his watch and sigh. Oh, good grief, I didn't know which was worse, him not coming to church or watching him cross his arms and sigh heavily.

As you can imagine, I continued to pray for Mike during this time. I asked God to help find someone to lead Mike to Christ. I needed a Christian husband. Our girls needed a Christian father. On and on went my prayers, until one night my conversation with God followed a different avenue. "Father, Mike needs you in his life. So forgive me for making my prayers all about me and my needs."

"The Lord is not slow in keeping his promise, as some understand slowness, instead he is patient with you, not wanting anyone to perish, but everyone to come to repentance." 2 Peter 3:9. I knew this verse included Mike. Accordingly, God's desire was for Mike to become a believer and have a relationship with him.

Catherine Marshall's <u>Something More</u>, 1974, explains what she calls the prayer of relinquishment. She had suffered from a medical condition for a year and a half. As you can imagine, she continually and desperately prayed for God to heal her to the point where she became mentally, emotionally, and spiritually exhausted. Catherine explained she had stopped demanding anything from God. Her prayer went on to confess that she only wanted what God wanted for her, even if that meant continued illness.

Catherine's prayer of relinquishment meant acceptance but also meant placing her deepest desire in God's capable hands. She no longer prayed for healing; she gave "it" to God. In doing so, a great burden was lifted from her. Simply put, Catherine came to a moment where she states, "I had touched the hem of His garment..." Praise God; later she was healed.

I praise God for writers like Catherine Marshall. By sharing their lives, they encourage and help many people, such as myself. After reading Something More, I tried to follow Christine's suggestion. Praying for Mike day after day, night after night had become an overwhelming burden. It was all-consuming.

God led me through hours of prayer one night when I finally said my own prayer of relinquishment. I confessed in my prayer that I knew God wanted what was best for Mike. After all, God created Mike; God brought us together. I surrendered my concern and anxiety for Mike and what I desired to happen. Believe me, I felt an immediate weight lifted from my shoulders! I asked God to help me focus on areas of my life that needed improvement and what parts of me should become more like Jesus?

The next Sunday, while Mike continued his "squirming," and we sang the invitation hymn, I prayed for others in attendance who might need to make a decision for Christ. I didn't pray for Mike to make a decision.

After a few months, John Eynon came over to our home for a visit. He was the young adult Bible teacher on Sunday mornings. This time when John asked Mike about his view of the Bible, I once again about fell out of my chair; but for a different reason than when Fred had first shared the gospel with Mike. The answer Mike gave John was he, Mike, had been reading the Bible. Really!? Wow! When? I didn't see him reading a Bible.

Mike asked John several in-depth questions. John was such a dynamic teacher. He brought God's word to life through his lessons. John had a great sense of humor and incorporated that skill into his lessons. His students were involved and encouraged.

One Sunday, early February 1976, Mike and I were once again standing during the invitation hymn. This time, Mike pulled on my belt and said, "Let me go." He wanted to get to the aisle so he could go down front and answer God's call to come to salvation. What a glorious day when Mike was baptized!

KEY BIBLE VERSE

Jeremiah 29:11
"'For I know the plans I have for you,' declares the Lord, 'plans to prosper you and not to harm you, plans to give you hope and a future.'"

In context, Jeremiah is addressing the exiles in Babylon. God's chosen people had been disobedient, and they were going to be punished. The Babylonians were planning to destroy Jerusalem and take the people into captivity. Jeremiah's words in verse 11 are meant to be encouraging. God would not forsake them. God's promise from the time of Abraham was that a messiah would come and be in the lineage of Abraham's son Isaac. Note, this promise to bring Israel back wasn't for all nations, just Israel.

"Jeremiah 29:11 has another application. In particular, this verse reflects a more general principle of God's grace and affections for those whom He loves, including the modern church. This more general application can be made because of the unchanging nature of God." Gotquestions.org

God has a plan for His children, a plan to give us hope and a future. He desires what is best for us, and through His

Word, we have directions for following His will. The verse in Jeremiah doesn't apply to all people, only those who have accepted God's call to salvation through Christ.

Another basic principle of God's goodness is shared in John chapter six, where Jesus performs the miracle of feeding the five thousand. In verses 12 and 13, "When they had all had enough to eat, He said to His disciples, 'Gather the pieces that are leftover. Let nothing be wasted.' So they gathered them and filled twelve baskets with the pieces of the five barley loaves left over by those who had eaten." Our God doesn't waste anything, anyone, any circumstance. He can and does use the "leftovers" for His good purpose.

Mike didn't come to know Jesus until he was thirty years old. Was his life before coming to God a waste? Certainly not. Once Mike went into ministry, God used all his life experiences to enhance his ministry. Because of Mike's background, military service, attending a large secular university, working for a business, all those experiences helped him relate to people in ways that only he could.

Dear friends, God will not waste any part of your life. Once you completely surrender to following Him and working to build His kingdom, God finds ways to use all of you, your past, your talents, your desires. Living in God's will and serving Him is what will make your life more fulfilling. Jesus says in John 10:10, "I have come that they may have life, and have it to the full." He created us; He knows us better than we know ourselves. Trust Him and be filled with true joy!

chapter seven

New City, New Life:
Bible College

Following Mike's baptism, our lives began to change. My life of trying to walk that fine line of not attending church too often was erased. Now every time the church doors were open, Mike said, "Let's go!" I certainly didn't object!

Sunday mornings, Sunday evenings, Wednesday night Bible study, fellowship dinners; we attended everything. Mike glowed with his excitement as he grew closer to the Lord. Many of our friends commented on how they could see the difference in Mike. I continued to float on air as I praised God for answering my prayers.

Without a doubt, we were "all in." On Sundays, we first attended John Eynon's young adult Bible class. During the second hour, I started volunteering to help teach the three-year-old class. At that same time, Mike signed up to help Mrs. Smith (Madonna) in the Children's church. Mike loved working with Madonna. Now he was learning basic Bible stories he had never heard or didn't remember from childhood.

During two years time, Mike grew by leaps and bounds in his relationship with Jesus, and he also grew in his knowledge of God's word. Then, as God would plan it, we had the unfathomable opportunity to attend the Florida Christian State conference, which took place in Jacksonville that year. These were the decades when the Christian Churches across the state of Florida would once a year gather for a conference. The goal was multi-purpose; encouraging each other to continue building the kingdom of God, learning and studying together, and experiencing worship of our God with thousands of people.

Because the state conference took place in the city where we lived, we could easily attend without the expense of a hotel. John Eynon was asked to present one of the workshops to share techniques and ideas on how to involve and engage young adults in Bible study. Unfortunately, at the last minute, John had to have emergency surgery and be in the hospital. Praise God it wasn't anything life-threatening. Fred Smith stepped in to cover for John. Then Fred asked Mike to co-present since Mike attended the classes. (Fred also taught a Bible class at church during the same time; therefore he hadn't seen John in action.)

Of course, I attended this session. What a joy to see Mike working with Fred, sharing ideas about teaching the Bible. Then, as we were visiting people after the workshop, two guys came up to us. After they introduced themselves, they asked Mike a question that blew me away; "Have you ever considered attending Bible college and becoming a preacher?"

These men were in their thirties and were attending Central Florida Bible College. They explained how they left their jobs when they decided to follow God's call into full-time ministry. Both men had families, and through God's grace, they were able to work at part-time jobs and go to classes.

Mike and I started wondering, "Was God also calling Mike?" We prayed together, asking God to direct us. In the back of my mind, I was thinking, whoa, God. I prayed for Mike to become a Christian, but this full-time thing?!? Plus, I explained to God, I can't be a preacher's wife! I can't sing or play the piano! In this time era, one expected stereotype was a preacher's wife was able to do both. She sang in the choir and or played the piano; I certainly didn't have any qualifications for that role.

During the weeks that followed, Mike continued to study God's word. Now that he was studying the Bible, he reevaluated his commitment to God. Mike has always been a very rational guy. Now, as he studied God's word, it was clear to him that it meant answering God's call.

We prayed with our church family at Englewood. Mike went to Fred Smith, John E=ynon, and others for advice. Finally, we both came to the same conclusion. God was calling Mike into full-time ministry.

At that time, Central Florida Bible College was located in Orlando. They were using the campus of First Christian Church. Later with God's blessings, the college was able to build a campus in Kissimmee. As years progressed, they changed their name to Florida Christian College. Present-day, the college has become part of Johnson University, with a campus in Knoxville, TN.

We initially decided to put our house up for sale in March of 1978. That is when I discovered that buying a new home in an older neighborhood had its drawbacks. Month after month went by, and no one was interested in our house. Each month we reduced the price, with no results. We had set a date in August to move to Orlando. Describing my feelings at the time would be easy, anxious!

I went to Orlando in search of a place to rent. Our plan was I would work full time, and Mike would attend college full time. (Hmm, sounds familiar, right?) One problem was Orlando had a housing shortage, especially for rentals. Some of the places I looked at required that we rent a three-bedroom place. I explained that we only needed a two-bedroom as we have two young daughters. No luck.

As weeks turned into months, I began to doubt our calling. One friend even kindly suggested that perhaps God was telling us not to go. But Mike was not deterred. God continued teaching us as we kept dropping our asking price for the house. It finally sold on the date we had planned to move!

After making a couple more trips to Orlando looking for housing, I was completely out of ideas. Finally, Fred told us he knew of someone with a rental house in Orlando, and we could stay there until we found a place. So, things seemed to be falling into place.

Our dear friends from church came over and helped us pack up a U-Haul truck. They had also provided us with a "pounding party," where they gave us plenty of food to stock up our pantry. The week prior, our church gave us a going away celebration with a "money tree." We were well-loved, supported, and prayed for.

So away we went early on that Saturday morning in August 1978, our girls, car, and possessions. Earlier, we had given away several furniture items. It seemed logical that wherever we landed, the space would be smaller than our current house.

A few hours later, we pulled into the parking lot of the church where the college was also housed. Once we called Fred's contact about the rental, we knew we had a problem. The house was no longer available! Now what?! We visited the college offices and shared our dilemma. One of the professors cheerfully invited us to spend a couple of nights with them.

Sunday morning was embarrassing, to say the least. During announcements, the preacher revealed to the congregation that the U-Haul truck they all noticed parked in the church's parking lot belongs to a young couple planning on attending Bible College, but they have nowhere to live. Mike and I sank as low as we could in the pew. Behind the caring looks of folks around us, we could imagine everyone thinking, "Who in their right mind would move to a new city without planning on where to live, and with two young children! How irresponsible!"

A Christian college is also like a church family. Therefore, we had an immediate support group, and several people helped search for a place to live. Unfortunately, each day that went by, the cost of the U-Haul increased. Finally, we found a house to rent, but even though it was a bit run down, it was really over the price we had planned in our budget. Remember, neither of us had a job at this time.

With a week to go before classes officially started, Mike quickly found a part-time job through someone at the college. It was construction work, but that was fine. I quickly searched for a job. These were the days of looking through the want ads in the newspaper.

Praise God; I found three openings for a keypunch/data entry operator. This skill had come in handy throughout our marriage. Each time I needed to get a job, I was quickly hired. My mind went back to the summer I attended the business school in Atlanta after high school graduation. At the time, I hated trying to speed up my time as I typed on those keys. How boring! Little did I know how useful this would be. Now I certainly saw God's hand in my life even then.

But this time, even with three different places with openings, I didn't get a job! What's going on, God?! Hey, did you forget we gave up everything to go into full-time ministry? (I think you can detect my whining.) Sincerely, I was confused and very anxious. Mike wasn't worried; he knew God would work something out.

We enrolled our girls in the nearby elementary school. The neighbors were very welcoming and glad to have someone in the house that had been vacant for a while. They even invited us to their neighborhood Labor Day celebration.

The date for our next month's rent was approaching, and I still didn't have a clue how we could manage paying the rent, electricity, water, etc.

That's when God stepped in through Fred Smith and his brother, Dr. James Smith (one of the professors at the college). The young couple doing the custodial jobs for the church and the college campus decided to get other jobs. That meant they would move out of the very small apartment that belonged to the college.

Subsequently, the college needed new custodians. Part of the arrangement with First Christian Church was the college provided custodians, which was reasonable since the classes were held in their building. Fred called and told us about the offer. We could move into the college apartment and work as custodians. We would earn a small salary, plus rent for the apartment was lower than any regular rental.

Fred added a very unexpected, unbelievable detail. Because our hours would be flexible, I would be able to attend classes!!! Furthermore, as the spouse of a full-time student, my enrollment fee would be reduced. I couldn't believe it! I had always wanted to go to college and now be able to attend a Bible college! Are you kidding me?!?!

To say that everything was smooth sailing after that would not just be an exaggeration; it would be a lie. Of course, our enemy came at us with both barrels. But as I mentioned, we had a strong support system, both at the college and from our "home" church, Englewood. Many times, just when I wondered how we would buy groceries for the week, I would go to the mailbox and find a check from someone.

Whenever Fred visited the college, he would stop by and look through our cabinets to make sure we had enough food. In addition, we received many "care packages" from several churches. (Side note, one time, we opened a package to find a rusty can of rutabagas! I didn't even open it.) You get the picture; through the grace and caring of God's people, we made ends meet.

Our four years at Central Florida Bible College were some of the most challenging and extraordinary times of our lives. Our girls lived in an atmosphere of loving, caring professors and families, and young people all striving to become the people God meant for them to be. What great examples they were!

KEY BIBLE VERSE

Isaiah 6:8
"Then I heard the voice of the Lord saying,
'Whom shall I send? And who will go for us?'
And I said, 'Here am I send me.'"

As I mentioned, once Mike began to read the Bible, he took it to heart. Isaiah was called to preach God's word during a desperate time in history. Our culture today is in dire need of the truth of God's word. If Mike answered God's call, it would mean leaving a job he liked that had a secure future, whereas going into ministry didn't guarantee a certain salary or pension. However, Mike has always been a committed person. When he tells someone he will do something; he follows through. Clearly, God needs preachers. God's word touched Mike's heart.

Paul states, "How, then, can they call on the one they have not believed in? And how can they believe in the one of whom they have not heard? And how can they hear without someone preaching to them?" Romans 10:14

We prayed together as a couple and as a family. We told our girls that we would be going into ministry as a family. I remember one time sitting at our extremely small kitchen table at Bible college, and Christie, who was about seven years old at the time, asked, "Can we just go where they don't have any cannibals?" I honestly don't know where Christie got that idea. But Mike answered in his usual style, "We won't because you are their favorite size."

During this time of my life, I understood the idea behind "full time" ministry meant only a few are "called" to serve in that capacity. I was wrong. Jesus said to his disciples, "All authority in heaven and on earth has been given to me. Therefore, go and make disciples of all nations, baptizing them in the name of the Father and of the Son and of the Holy Spirit, and teaching them to obey everything I have commanded you. And surely, I am with you always, to the very end of the age." Matthew 28:18-20

Originally, I thought this passage was just meant for the disciples Jesus was speaking to before his ascension. Then as I studied more carefully, it occurred to me that when Jesus says, "teaching them to obey everything I have commanded you," it would mean passing His commands down through the generations. Therefore, we are all called to make disciples, baptize them, and teach them. Amazingly, that is how His church has continued throughout history. We are all responsible!

"Full-time" ministry is a unique calling, but it is meant for all Christians. Yes, you may have a five-day-a-week job working for a company or business, but you are still considered a disciple of Christ telling others the Good News.

chapter eight

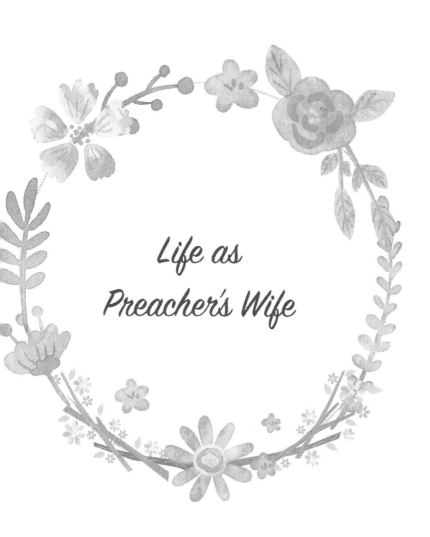

*Life as
Preacher's Wife*

As much as I learned during our time at Bible College, I was still not fully prepared for what we would face in real-life ministry. With rose-colored glasses, I thought God must truly protect His full-time servants. After all, they were giving their entire lives to building His kingdom, so God must give them extra protection and guidance.

Yes, God guided us and protected us, but the enemy's arrows came from unexpected places. Too many times, Satan would use some of the people in God's church to attack. Sometimes we felt like the walking wounded.

In our first ministry, we were so excited to be working in a church. My enthusiasm was high because, after all, God gave me the unimaginable blessing of attending Bible College. I passionately wanted to share what I had the privilege of learning. My degree was in Christian education. I went to work teaching on Sundays, first hour Bible study, second-hour Children's Church, Sunday evening kids' Bible class. On Wednesday evening, while Mike taught adult Bible study, I taught the children's class.

My picture of ministry was that I would invite someone to come alongside me and learn some of the things I had learned. Then they would lead their own class. Silly me! Everyone was perfectly happy with me doing it all–no need for them to get involved.

Of course, I jumped into the women's ministry and joined them for their meetings and Bible study. At one of the first meetings, the ladies were discussing someone who was not in attendance. They felt she was doing something wrong. One woman turned to me and said, "Well, let's ask the new preacher's wife what she thinks." Oh boy, now what?

I turned to Matthew 18:15-17, thinking it was a safe bet, quoting Jesus. "If your brother or sister sins, go and point out their fault, just between the two of you. If they listen to you, you have won them over. But if they will not listen, take one or two others along so that 'every matter may be established by the testimony of two or three witnesses.' If they still refuse to listen, tell it to the church." The ladies just nodded.

Later that week, word got back to me that I told the women to get the elders to kick the woman out of church! This "news" traveled so far that we heard from the preacher and his wife that lived in the next town. They told us that some people were saying that the new preacher's wife was causing a lot of trouble!

All along, Mike stayed calm and continued to preach God's word. I admired his faithfulness and total commitment to God's work remaining true to the Bible. This was a small country church with a well-established membership. Unknown to us when we arrived, there was underlying division in the congregation. Many families that lived here had been in the area for generations. As human nature would have it, one family did not approve of another.

Someone in one family would come to Mike's office and explain that he should direct his preaching to the other family. Then someone in the other family would do the same. But, again, Mike was not deterred. He simply preached God's word. You get the picture; Mike couldn't please anyone. But I have no doubt Mike pleased God because Mike stayed true to God's word.

My "they lived happily ever after" mindset was quickly erased, and it finally came to the point where we had to leave. Even with God's help, we were not able to heal the division in the congregation. In a few years, we were living with my sweet Grandmother in Tampa and praying for God to reveal where He wanted us to go next. We both got jobs, and Mike sent out resumes, many resumes.

After about six months, we heard of a small church in central Florida in need of a preacher, and a date was set for us to visit. Mike prepared his "trial" sermon. As we got acquainted with people, it was mentioned that the congregation had voted <u>out</u> all of their Elders, the past Sunday! That sent red flags off in my mind. We prayed about the situation, and Mike felt that he might help this church body heal. My feelings told me to <u>run</u>!

Once again, it became clear that Mike's preaching couldn't please everybody, but that was not his purpose. Mike stayed true to God's word and could disciple several men. It was a joy to watch as some of the men came to Mike for guidance and direction on becoming better servants of Christ.

My ministry continued with the children. As I had experienced in our previous church, once again, I was teaching all the kids' classes. Come Sunday morning I first taught during Bible school hour, the second hour, I taught Children's Church, on Sunday nights I taught the kids' class and on Wednesday evening. Even though this didn't fit my vision of ministry, I loved teaching the kids. Sure, I was worn out, but the Lord provided joy through the children as they learned about Jesus.

One bonus, this location was within 90 miles of the University of Central Florida in Orlando. I was able, with God's protection and guidance, to enter a master's program there. Initially, I did substitute teaching during the day and attended classes at night. Wow! What a challenge!

Attending a sizable secular college was an immense awakening to a different reality. At Bible College, the student body was small, about one hundred at the time we attended. On the other hand, Central Florida was a huge campus with a student body of more than 50,000! Plus, many on staff, including the professors, didn't show any concern whether or not the students succeeded.

I was required to take two classes initially, making a grade of "A" or "B" to be allowed into the master's program. The first class dealt with social issues that affect education. After the first test, I was struggling. I went to the professor to ask for help and offered to do extra work to help my grade. His response was, "Considering where you came from (meaning a small Christian college), you don't even need to show up for the final." I walked out in shock, but God gave me the strength to continue, and I managed to receive a "B" in the class.

My first trip to the campus library was weird and strange for me. (Unfortunately for many today, going to any library might seem like a weird or strange experience. It is much easier to just ask Google.) Mike had encouraged me to "just act like you know what you are doing." So, I walked what seemed like a mile or more to the large library building. I marched in, just like I knew where I was going. I found the card catalog (okay, look that up on Google.) A nice young man came over to explain that the university used the Library of Congress system, not the Dewey Decimal system. He quickly spouted out the numbers and what they meant. I told him the topic I was interested in researching, and he kindly told me to go to the <u>fourth</u> floor.

Not seeing an elevator nearby, I decided I could take the stairs. As I opened the door on the next floor, all I saw were periodicals. Hmm, and then I saw a sign that said, "<u>3rd floor</u>." What?!?! What happened to the second floor?? That was it; my "cool, calm" façade was about to collapse into tears. I somewhat calmly turned around, went down the stairs, and marched toward the front door, at which time I saw a huge cube with the number two on it. You entered the library on the second floor! What kind of place is this?

Pulling myself together as much as possible, I continued to exit the door. A young man was at the exit area and politely asked me if I would like an escort to my car. I quickly said, "No, thank you," and rushed on. It was probably about nine o'clock or later. As I hurriedly walked to the parking lot, which must be about 3 miles away, I thought to myself, do I need an escort?!?

Once again, I praise God for Mike's support. The following Saturday, we drove back to the university. We walked to the library building, and he helped me find the materials I needed. After being accepted into the master's program, I was hired as a full-time teacher. I had 18 months left in the master's program, but with Mike's encouragement and God's protection, I made it.

This led to a 32-year career of teaching in public elementary schools. Now I had another "ministry field" the children in my class and many of my co-workers.

As a public-school teacher, I found ways to share Jesus. For example, at Christmas, I always put up a small nativity scene. (I made sure I also decorated with a small Menorah In case some children were Jewish.) Reading aloud time was part of our day. What joy to see the children's faces as I read classics like James and the Giant Peach and The Lion, the Witch, and the Wardrobe. At Christmas, I read a picture book with a paraphrase of Luke 2. It amazed me the number of children who had never heard the story of the birth of Jesus.

During my career, I had the opportunity to teach in many different schools. My goal was to make sure each of my students knew that God loved them, and so did I, and that would never change. The times I was able to stay at one school for several years, many children would come back to visit me as they moved on to upper grades. I was always ready with a hug, and "I still love you, and so does God."

Although we found ministry in the churches we served very challenging, we also received many blessings. In each place we served, God was in control. He continued to teach both of us through the trials and blessings.

KEY BIBLE VERSE

Philippians 1:6
*"Paul said, 'being confident of this, that he
who began a good work in you will carry it on
to completion until the day of Christ Jesus.'"*

Paul's words are so encouraging. He was promising the church at Philippi that their work would not be in vain. God will bring it to completion. That holds true for us. Mike and I realized that even though it seemed like our ministries were failures or certainly not what we expected, God blessed our efforts to build His kingdom.

In Philippians 2:13 Paul states, "for it is God who works in you to will and act in order to fulfill his good purpose." We know His purpose is for all to come to a saving knowledge of Jesus. What joy we experience when we are being used by God for His good work.

Paul's advice is more difficult to follow, in verses 14-15. "Do everything without grumbling or arguing so that you may become blameless and pure, 'children of God without fault in a warped and crooked generation.' Then you will shine among them like stars in the sky."

I would like to say that in our ministries, Mike and I were able to hold Paul's instruction, but that wouldn't be true. Certainly, we had times of grumbling, complaining, and arguing, although the church family didn't see or hear us, at least for the most part. Along with the grumbling, we also experienced doubt and hurt. Often, I asked God why? We were doing our best to bring to His church unity and love for one another.

Scripture instructs us and reassures us. Ecclesiastes 11:1 "Cast your bread upon the waters, for you will find it after many days." Commentators explain that Solomon is referring to doing good works, "but the one who sows righteousness reaps a sure reward." Proverbs 18b and "let us not become weary in doing good, for at the proper time we will reap a harvest if we do not give up." Galatians 6:9.

As we analyzed the problems that faced us, each time it was evident who was behind our difficulties, "For our struggle is not against flesh and blood, but against the rulers, against the authorities, against the powers of this dark world and against the spiritual forces of evil in the heavenly realms." Ephesians 6:12

Sarah Young describes our Christian walk so well, "Anticipate coming face-to-face with impossibilities: situations totally beyond your ability to handle. This awareness of your inadequacy is not something you should try to evade. It is precisely where I want you—the best place to encounter Me in *My Glory and Power*. When you see armies of problems marching toward you, cry out to Me! Allow Me to fight for you. Watch Me working on your behalf, as you *rest in the shadow of My Almighty Presence*." <u>Jesus Calling</u>, 2004, page 241.

My dear friends, heed Paul's words as he describes putting on the full armor of God in Ephesians chapter six."

Finally, be strong in the Lord and in His mighty power. Put on the full armor of God, so that you can take your stand against the devil's schemes. For our struggle is not against flesh and blood, but against the rulers, against the authorities, against the powers of this dark world and against the spiritual forces of evil in the heavenly realms. Therefore, put on the full armor of God, so that when the day of evil comes, you may be able to stand your ground, and after you have done everything, to stand. Stand firm then, with the belt of truth buckled around your waist, with the breastplate of righteousness in place, and with your feet fitted with the readiness that comes from the gospel of peace. In addition to all this, take up the shield of faith, with which you can extinguish all the flaming arrows of the evil one. Take the helmet of Salvation and the sword of the Spirit, which is the word of God. And pray in the Spirit on all occasions with all kinds of prayers and requests. With this in mind, be alert and always keep on praying for the Lord's people. (Verses 11 – 18)

God gives us all the necessary equipment we need to fight the devil and the powers of this dark world. All we must do is use these tools: God's truth, His righteousness, be ready at all times to share the gospel with love and peace. Our faith, knowing the Holy Spirit that lives within us, is much stronger than anything flaming arrows of the evil one. Our sword is God's Holy Word. It is sharper than any two-edged sword. So, finally, before, during, and after Satan's attacks: <u>pray</u>.

My dear friends, we stand together as one mighty army marching into the spiritual battle we face in our culture today. Be on guard, "Be alert and of sober mind. Your enemy, the devil prowls around like a roaring lion looking for someone to devour." I Peter 5:8. But we get the last laugh, we are victorious in Christ Jesus our Lord!

chapter nine

Mission to Haiti

After leaving our ministry in middle Florida, we decided to move back to Fort Myers. This seemed reasonable as we could live in an extra house that belonged to Mike's parents for very low rent. Time to catch our breath and pray about what would come next.

I started working at an elementary school across town. Immediately, I liked the administration and the teachers in my grade level. Planning together was motivating and exciting. (a side note: during this particular year, the state government's budget was tight, so there was a freeze on hiring new teachers. Although I had five years of teaching experience, by moving to a new county, I would be considered a "new" hire. But God provided a school with a principal that hired me anyway!)

We barely started the school year when Mike received a call from Fred Smith. He knew we were between ministries. Fred had a proposal for Mike. The Englewood church had always been very active in supporting Christianville in Haiti. This mission planted churches and started schools for the Haitian people. In fact, at this time, they had five churches (some tiny) but in each location was also a school. The only way most of the Haitian children could go to school was through a benevolent organization. Their government doesn't provide free grade schools.

Fred explained that they needed someone knowledgeable with computers who could teach the young Haitian preachers. The computer duties included setting up a better management system for tracking the fundraising done through churches in the States. People from all over the United States would sponsor a child at Christianville. The funds would cover food, materials, and medical care for the children.

Mike was just the man. He knew how to operate personal computers and set up the accounting programs needed. And, of course, he was also very knowledgeable about the Bible and loved the idea of helping the Haitian preachers.

He called me at school and explained that he was going to Haiti next <u>week</u>. This would just be a trial period to see if he was a good fit. If it was, Mike would stay for several months. Okay, pause; what should I do? As I mentioned before, Mike is strong on being true to a commitment. I had already signed a contract for the school year. That meant that I would stay in Fort Myers and continue teaching through that school year.

Even as a child, I dreamed of being a missionary. Upon reflection, my mind certainly romanticized what that kind of commitment would genuinely mean. While we attended Bible college, every time the school had a visiting missionary preach in Chapel, I wanted to run home and pack my bags. Their plea for workers always touched my heart. The idea of accepting a call to be missionaries had entered our minds many times, but Haiti?

When I got home that night, Mike was so excited he could hardly speak. Finally, someone needed him, needed his particular skills and talents! Hadn't we been praying for where God wanted us to serve next? My head was still spinning. To describe Mike as thrilled wouldn't give the full picture. He was elated! He shared his conversation with Fred in more detail. They would provide Mike with a plane ticket for the next week. The plan was for Mike to stay at Christianville and get acquainted with the entire operation.

Over the years, as Christianville developed, the mission grew. They built several buildings consisting of the main house that could house 20 or more people, a large two-story school building, a church building for worship, a medical clinic, clinics for visiting dentists and eye doctors, plus a working farm. In addition, they had cows, pigs, goats, a fishpond, a large section for crops, mainly vegetables. With the sponsor a child program, which included hundreds of children, the entire operation was large and complex.

The next thing I knew, Mike was on a plane heading to Haiti. Phone service was spotty, but when he did call, I could tell in his voice how much he loved the work and the people. He stayed for a month; then he came home. We had a few months together, including Christmas. During that time, our goal focused on raising funds for our ministry.

Our churches have a basic procedure for missionaries, whether in the US or overseas. Each person must raise their own support. This means traveling to different churches and asking for donations and/or monthly support. Let me be clear; this process is not fun. You feel like you are on "display" and presenting evidence of why you deserve to get money from people. As always, God is faithful, and we were blessed. After Christmas, Mike returned to Christianville with the plan that I would visit during my school spring break.

On the one hand, it seemed like the perfect time to serve in a foreign country. On the other hand, both of our girls were attending Florida Christian College. Accordingly, Mike and I were experiencing the "empty nest" syndrome. When we explained our plans to them, they were certainly supportive. Although Melinda did state, "You better come home because I'm not going to visit you in Haiti!" She heard about the tarantulas!

Spring break came, and my first visit to Haiti was filled with new experiences, new people, and culture shock. Haiti is the most impoverished nation in the Western Hemisphere.

Seeing pictures is one thing, but undoubtedly it is nothing compared to being there.

To be respectful of their culture, women from the mission wore skirts. If a woman had pants or shorts on, that indicated a certain lifestyle which we didn't represent. So, when Mike picked me up from the airport, my first challenge was climbing into the high pick-up truck with a skirt on. Immediately my senses were inundated with sights, sounds and smells that I will never forget. Port-a-Prince is a crowded city with loud noises, no working traffic lights, and rotting trash. Very few roads were paved; most were dirt with huge potholes. I sat next to Mike and just grinned as my head and body bounded all over the small cab of the truck, no seat belts!

Christianville is located in the countryside. The main house compound is surrounded by high walls. Outside the walls was a small village of mud huts. One of the missionaries who had been there several years showed me around. As we walked through the village, the people would wave and smile. I asked many questions, why don't they do this or that. One reality that hit me over and over, no electricity meant no refrigeration. If a family got a chicken, they cooked it and shared the meal with the community. Otherwise, rice and beans were cooked over a fire daily.

During my week's visit, I went with Kathy (she and her husband had been working there for a couple of years) and two other visiting ladies to the market in the nearest town. Imagine four blanche (white) women walking down the dirt road to a somewhat paved road to get on a Taptap (look it up on Google). These small pickup trucks were converted to carry at least thirty people or more. They were covered with wood sections painted various bright multi-colors. Down each side of the bed of the truck, they had wooden planks to sit on.

We adamantly told Kathy, make sure we all could get on the same Taptap. She was the only one who could speak Creole. Of course, we "stood out" from the others waiting for the next ride. One Taptap zoomed (just because the roads were narrow and poorly paved didn't slow down their speed) into the stop. It was full! I mean full! When we looked into the back of the truck, both side benches were full. Haitians were shoulder to shoulder, and their knees met in the middle.

One man jumped off the truck and must have said, "No worries!" in Creole. Kathy was explaining that we all wanted to be on the same Taptap. All the while, he helped her get in and sit on a tiny saw-horse-type stool between the knees of the people already on the truck. Next was a friend, again helped on by the man. She turned and sat with her back to Kathy, who was now facing the cab with her nose to the window. Then the man helped me on. Remember we were all wearing skirts. We had to bend over to lower our heads to get into the Taptap. Picture this; I'm bent over, my rear-end is somewhat sticking out. I quickly surmise that my choices are to sit on my friend's lap or sit on a Haitian's lap. I started to turn around when someone grabbed my rear (No kidding!) and placed it on another miniature stool. Where it came from, I'll never know! As the Taptap pulled out onto the road and my face was now as red as my skirt; all the Haitians were laughing. I asked Kathy what they were saying, and she explained that I didn't want to know.

After my brief visit, I returned to Fort Myers and finished the next few months of teaching school. All the while, I was preparing and packing for a 12-month stay in Haiti. During my initial visit, I was introduced to what my basic responsibilities would be: hostess for the main house to prepare for visiting teams was the biggest job. As I explained, Christianville is a working farm. They raised cows, goats, and pigs. Many vegetables came from their fields. Other basic food items came from the grocery store in Port-a-Prince. Finally, each person who came with a team from the States was asked to bring an extra piece of luggage with food, such as canned goods, cake mixes, pudding, etc. Items not found in Haiti.

Upon my arrival, I was inundated with people and issues that needed immediate attention. Another team of workers from the States was arriving the next day. With the help of the Haitians that worked at the main house (only one spoke English) and a beautiful woman called Auntie (originally from Jamaica, who spoke with a heavy accent and was mostly blind and in her eighties), I needed to quickly make a grocery list. One of the workers would then go into the city and buy the groceries. My adjustment to the extreme poverty and culture needed to be pushed aside.

Making a grocery list to accommodate 15 people who would be staying a week was a daunting task, especially since I was completely out of place on a <u>working farm</u>. To get vegetables and other items; it was required that I go into the walk-in cooler, which had <u>hanging meat</u>! This was another new experience for me. My duties included going downstairs to the large freezer and selecting the meat for the Haitian cook to prepare. The freezer was full of "chucks" of some kind of meat wrapped multiple times. None of the "chucks" were labeled! Upon inspection, I could identify the chicken; it was small. The other larger pieces—could be beef or pork, and who knows how many pounds. This "dilemma" led to the dinner conversation: "Pam, what kind of meat is this?" My answer, "Roast."

As much as Mike was qualified for the duties he needed to accomplish, I was unqualified. Planning three meals a day for 10 to 25 people was a challenge. Add the complexity of a working farm, explaining to a Haitian cook who didn't speak English, what to cook, deciding how much rice, beans, etc., was needed for each meal. I was barely holding my head above water.

Let me emphasize, the Haitian people were wonderful. Most of the people we worked with were Christians. When visiting teams came in, many times, the young Haitians would ask, "Do you know Jesus? He is my Life!" The times I worked with the schools and teachers were highlights for me. Even with the necessity of having an interpreter, I loved teaching.

Besides the challenges of living surrounded by poverty, language barriers, lacking cooking skills, being on a working farm, no air conditioning (I know I'm spoiled), the major difficulty for me was, I missed our girls. Sure, they were doing well in school, and we were proud of what they were doing and the goals they had set, but my heart ached to see them. I was lonely. Mike worked throughout the day into the evenings. We worked and lived at the main house. In the evenings, I could go over and watch him in the office work or sit in our room and read.

After about five months, a military coup took place. The president was ousted, and the army took control. Young Haitian men were taken from their homes and enlisted into the army; therefore, all the schools closed. The American Ambassador in Port-a-Prince told Americans to get out of the country and, if they did stay, "Keep a low profile."

I had experienced stomach issues since my arrival. The well Christianville used for the water supply was tested and confirmed "safe," but not so much for me. Thank the Lord this problem wasn't terribly debilitating, just inconvenient. Right after the coup, I developed an ear infection. Going to a Haitian hospital and doctor is another story. Add to those factors, the schools closed, and visiting teams couldn't come to Haiti; Mike decided that I needed to go home.

Thus, my time as a missionary ended. Mike stayed at Christianville. He was determined to keep the mission open and fulfill our commitment to stay for a year.

KEY BIBLE VERSE

Matthew 25:21
"His master replied, 'Well done, good and faithful servant! You have been faithful with a few things; I will put you in charge of many things. Come and share your master's happiness!'"

Mike's life is a strong example of staying true to your commitment. Once he read the Bible and became a Christian, his goal was to fulfill his purpose in Christ. Whether it was our call to a local ministry or Haiti, Mike's focus was sharp. Preach God's word and remain faithful. This included the difficult times and obstacles. For myself, I often found difficulty in staying focused on God's purpose.

I certainly wasn't a "happy camper" returning to Florida without Mike. But, praise God; I was able to see a doctor right away and get the medicine needed to heal my ear infection. Obviously, my next step was finding a teaching position.

Once again, the state government put a freeze on hiring new teachers.

The school year was well underway, as this was November. Thank goodness the schools always need substitute teachers. My first opportunity to sub was in the school that I had worked at the previous year. The principal that I liked and respected was still there, and when she heard I was available for subbing, she gave me that opening. This was a class of 31 first graders! In addition, I found out that they needed an extended sub. The teacher who started the school year with this class decided to move back north.

At the end of my first day, the principal called me into her office, and explained the situation. Then she asked if I would be willing to serve as an "extended sub" for this particular class (interestingly, it was located in the same room where I taught the previous year). The caveat was substitute pay was a lot less than teacher pay, but as an extended sub, I would have all the duties and responsibilities of a full-time teacher. Of course, I agreed. Now that I was back in the States, I needed an income.

As much as I praised God for the quick job opening, I continued to be confused and a bit lost. We had followed God's lead by going to Haiti. While Mike was very successful at completing the tasks that were needed; I felt like a failure. I was not a "good fit" for being hostess of the Mission House. In fact, I was "a mess!" Add to that; I wasn't doing anything to tell others about Jesus, especially since I couldn't speak Creole, even with taking classes! But to come home without Mike?

Psalm 119:105, "Your word is a lamp for my feet, and a light on my path." I couldn't see the road ahead. I didn't like the circumstances I found myself in, *__but__* I continued to lean on God.

After a few months, my principal again called me into her office. She explained that she had a meeting with the school board and explained that I should be hired back as a full-time teacher. Part of her justification was that I had taken a year's leave of absence and not fully resigned. Even with the state department of education having a hiring freeze, I was given a new contract as a full-time teacher. Therefore, I had full pay and health insurance. After her good news, I remember very enthusiastically saying to my principal, "With God and Mrs. Benner on your side, great things happen!"

Mike was fulfilling his commitment to God and His purpose; now, I was also being used by God to build His kingdom.

What about you, dear friend? What "talents" has God entrusted you with? We all have gifts or talents. Romans 12:6-8, "We have different gifts, according to the grace given to each of us. If your gift is prophesying, then prophesy in accordance with your faith; if it is serving, then serve; if it is teaching, then teach; if it is to encourage, then give encouragement; if it is giving, then give generously; if it is to lead, do it diligently; if it is to show mercy, do it cheerfully."

As I explained, we don't always like the circumstances we find ourselves in, but God expects us to be faithful servants. Throughout our lives, situations change, circumstances change. Whatever conditions you might be facing right now in your life, God has a plan and a purpose for you.

I am sure that no matter where you live or what job you might have, you share my goal of someday wanting to hear

God our Father say, "Well done, good and faithful servant! You have been faithful with a few things; I will put you in charge of many things. Come and share your master's happiness!'" Matthew 25:21.

chapter ten

*Full Circle,
Looking Back*

At this point in my life, it is natural to reflect on events of my past. As the saying goes, "Hindsight is 20/20." It is much easier to see how God's plan for our lives unfolded by looking back. No matter how many times I stumbled or even strayed from God's path, He held me in His arms. He helped me get up or find my way back to Him.

God's continued faithfulness and His multitude of blessings throughout our lives are my main motivators for writing this book. Luke 12:48, "From everyone who has been given much, much will be demanded; and from the one who has been entrusted with much, much more will be asked." My desire to praise God and share the joy He can give developed into seeking the best way to tell people.

To specifically list the blessings God has given Mike and me, would fill volumes. Beyond the priceless gift of salvation through Christ, He graced us with our two daughters, sons-in-law, and five grandchildren. Through the people at Englewood Christian Church, He led Mike to Christ. This, in turn, led us to go to Bible college. At that point, although it was beyond my wildest dreams, God provided a way for me to also attend college.

The passion God placed in my heart as a child was fulfilled through being a preacher's wife and becoming a public-school teacher. Time after time, I had the opportunity to share the love of Jesus, and in turn, show Christ how much I love Him. My prayer is that someday many of the children I taught will meet me in Heaven.

Reflecting on my life, I am reminded of the many scriptures that encouraged me and guided me. 2 Corinthians 3:18, "And we all, who with unveiled faces contemplate the Lord's glory, are being transformed into his image with ever-increasing glory, which comes from the Lord, who is the

Spirit." Now I see more clearly how God's word is transforming me, so I continue to become more like Christ. This process will continue until He calls me home.

Through more than 50 years of marriage, mixed in with our blessings, we have dealt with heartaches, and at times, grief. Once again, we found comfort in God's word. "The Lord is close to the brokenhearted and saves those who are crushed in spirit." Psalm 34:18. "Brothers and sisters, we do not want you to be uninformed about those who sleep in death, so that you do not grieve like the rest of mankind, who have no hope. For we believe that Jesus died and rose again, and so we believe that God will bring with Jesus those who have fallen asleep in him." 1 Thessalonians 4:13-14.

One passage that has brought comfort on numerous occasions throughout my life is Philippians 4:6-8. "Do not be anxious about anything, but in every situation, by prayer and petition, with thanksgiving, present your requests to God. And the peace of God, which transcends all understanding, will guard your hearts and your minds in Christ Jesus." I would read this passage over and over. This is one of my favorite scriptures to share with others when they are facing trials. Whether I was facing some kind of surgery or Mike was having an operation, I repeated these verses. I found that when I turned God's word into a prayer, I did receive His peace. One word at a time, do not be anxious about anything. I checked several versions of the Bible. They all have the same meaning. "Anything," whether it is a minute concern or a critical situation. Next call on God through prayer and petition. The next phrase stands out, "with thanksgiving." In many incidents I needed to search for what to be thankful about. But God acknowledges our thankful hearts, and He will give us His peace.

God's word, His living word, guides us, "...all scripture is God-breathed and is useful for teaching, rebuking, correcting and training in righteousness," 2 Timothy 3:16. Just think about it, God provided salvation through Christ and continued guidance through His word. Plus, we have God's gift of His Holy Spirit. Over and over, I have learned to read and study His Word more diligently. Then I ask the Holy Spirit to guide me throughout my day, so I may be used for God's purpose.

Romans 12:2, "Do not conform to the pattern of this world but be transformed by the renewing of your mind. Then you will be able to test and approve what God's will is-His good and pleasing and perfect will." The only way we can follow God's plan for our lives is by following His Word. When you come to a situation where you are in doubt as to what to do or say, pray for the Holy Spirit to guide you. He will. Once you experience being a servant of God, you are filled with indescribable joy.

The first place to start serving God is through His church. God, our creator, knows what we need even before we do. He created us as social beings in need of relationships, connections with others. He created the family unit and designed His church to function as a family.

The relationships I have developed through God's church family are a foreshadow of what Heaven will be like. Scott Brennan gives us a perfect example by describing the relationship between Mary and Elizabeth, Luke 1:42-45.

"Mary is troubled and needs a friend to help her make sense of what has happened. Elizabeth is in tune with what God is doing because she confirms and encourages what Mary knew. Soul friendship is not about being directive but affirming what God is already doing. It is a ministry of encouragement. It offers support in times of trouble and celebration. Mary stayed with Elizabeth for three months. Hospitality is at the heart of soul friendship. It could be coffee around the kitchen table or a bed for an extended stay."

"Mary and Elizabeth had already laid the foundation for soul friendship. This is good practice. Make soul friendship normal and established so that in times of trouble, it has greater stability. Soul friends come from surprising places and could be a member of the family or someone who shares similar experiences. Pray and seek a soul friend; it is a beautiful part of the spiritual journey." Scott Brennan, devotion on FB 11/22/2021

Dear friends, we are all running the race set before us by God. "Therefore, since we are surrounded by such a great cloud of witnesses, let us throw off everything that hinders and the sin that so easily entangles. And let us run with perseverance the race marked out for us." Hebrews 12:1.

Christ's church needs an A-Team. Some of you might remember the '80's television show with four men who were former Army Special Forces. Each show featured the team tackling what seemed like an impossible task to save someone or right a wrong. Each of the four characters had a specialized talent, and when they all worked together, the "plan" would be successful.

God gave each of us specialized talents to be used for His plan. When we work as a team, we see success. Our task may seem impossible as we face a mighty enemy, but our God is stronger. So, dear friends, put on the armor God gave each of us, and let's work as an A-Team to defeat Satan's plan.

I'M A MESS

My prayer is that by sharing small scenes of my life and explaining how God stayed faithful, you are encouraged in your walk with our Lord.

End Notes

Chapter 1, Page 6
- From Dobson's article, June 2021, https://www.drjamesdobson.org/newsletters/june-newsletter-2021

Chapter 3, Page 14
- From Scott Brennan, Coach at Cairn Movement, Scotland, devotion 11/2/2021, https://www.facebook.com/scott.brennan.397/posts/10225323344006022

Chapter 4, Page 49
- Morgan, Marabel; Total Woman, 1973, Revell Publisher

Chapter 6, Page 70
- From the article What is the meaning of "for I know the plans I have for you" in Jeremiah 29:11? https://www.gotquestions.org/Jeremiah-29-11.html

Chapter 8, Page 39
- Young, Sarah; Jesus Calling, 2004, page 241, Thomas Nelson publisher

Chapter 10, Page 49
- From Scott Brennan, devotion on FB 11/22/2021, https://www.facebook.com/scott.brennan.397/posts/10225451176841763

Acknowledgments

Thank You

- First and foremost to our Lord and Savior, Jesus Christ.

- To Michael, always by my side and encouraging me throughout this project.

- To Carol Melcer and Patti McGiven, my first readers, who gave me suggestions and encouragement.

- To Jessica Conley, Jodi Costa, Kenzie Koltz, Sarah Williams, and the entire Two Penny Publishing team.

- To my sisters-Christ at Rise Christian Church, who so graciously allow me to study God's word with them, pray with them, and encourage each other.

About the Author

Pamela Davidson is a wife, mother, grandmother, and most importantly devoted follower of Christ. She and her husband, Michael, are both Florida "natives" and they continue to live in Florida where they will soon celebrate 55 years of marriage. Pam and Mike are blessed with two daughters, and sons-in-law, and five grandchildren.

Pam attended Central Florida Bible College (also known as Florida Christian College, now Johnson University of FL) with her husband. She received a bachelor's degree in Christan Education, and he earned a bachelor's degree in Preaching Ministry.

As they began their first local ministry, Pam started teaching in the elementary schools. She continued her education by attending the University of Central Florida, receiving a master's degree in elementary education. After 32 years working in public schools, Pam retired.

During her career Pam created many educational workshops presenting them at local reading events, the Florida State Reading Conference, and the International Reading Conference. She was president of the county-wide Reading Council.

Pam's passion for teaching and sharing God's love continues as she leads Bible studies at her local church. Plus, she has presented workshops at the state women's retreat.

Made in the USA
Columbia, SC
17 July 2022

63527927R00070